# Charlotta BASS

1607

CALIFORNIA EAGLE

ESTABLISHED 1879

PRINTERS PUBLISHERS LINOTYPER

BY J. P. MILLER

ILLUSTRATED BY
AMANDA QUARTEY

Rourke
Educational Media

A Division of
Carson
Dellosa
Education

## Before Reading: *Building Background Knowledge and Vocabulary*

Building background knowledge can help children process new information and build upon what they already know. Before reading a book, it is important to tap into what children already know about the topic. This will help them develop their vocabulary and increase their reading comprehension.

## Questions and Activities to Build Background Knowledge:

1. Look at the front cover of the book and read the title. What do you think this book will be about?
2. What do you already know about this topic?
3. Take a book walk and skim the pages. Look at the table of contents, photographs, captions, and bold words. Did these text features give you any information or predictions about what you will read in this book?

## Vocabulary: *Vocabulary Is Key to Reading Comprehension*

Use the following directions to prompt a conversation about each word.

- Read the vocabulary words.
- What comes to mind when you see each word?
- What do you think each word means?

### Vocabulary Words:
- *accused*
- *brutality*
- *convention*
- *discrimination*
- *journalism*
- *movement*
- *nomination*
- *policy*

## During Reading: *Reading for Meaning and Understanding*

To achieve deep comprehension of a book, children are encouraged to use close reading strategies. During reading, it is important to have children stop and make connections. These connections result in deeper analysis and understanding of a book.

 Close Reading a Text

During reading, have children stop and talk about the following:

- Any confusing parts
- Any unknown words
- Text to text, text to self, text to world connections
- The main idea in each chapter or heading

Encourage children to use context clues to determine the meaning of any unknown words. These strategies will help children learn to analyze the text more thoroughly as they read.

When you are finished reading this book, turn to the next-to-last page for **Text-Dependent Questions** and an **Extension Activity**.

# TABLE OF CONTENTS

# A WINNER EITHER WAY

Have you ever wanted to change a rule that seemed unfair? Have you worked with others to make a change? Charlotta Bass helped others by fighting for **policy** changes. She got people in the United States to fix important problems.

Charlotta looked over the top of her wire-rim glasses into the crowd. There were laws that kept Black people from entering most buildings, but she stood proudly on the **convention** stage in Chicago, Illinois. She was there to accept the Progressive Party's 1952 **nomination** for vice president. She could have the second-highest office in the United States government.

After the convention, Charlotta took her campaign on the road. She enabled Black people to talk about issues in their communities. She spoke about ways to change the rules and help people. When discussing the election, she told people, "Win or lose, we win by raising the issues."

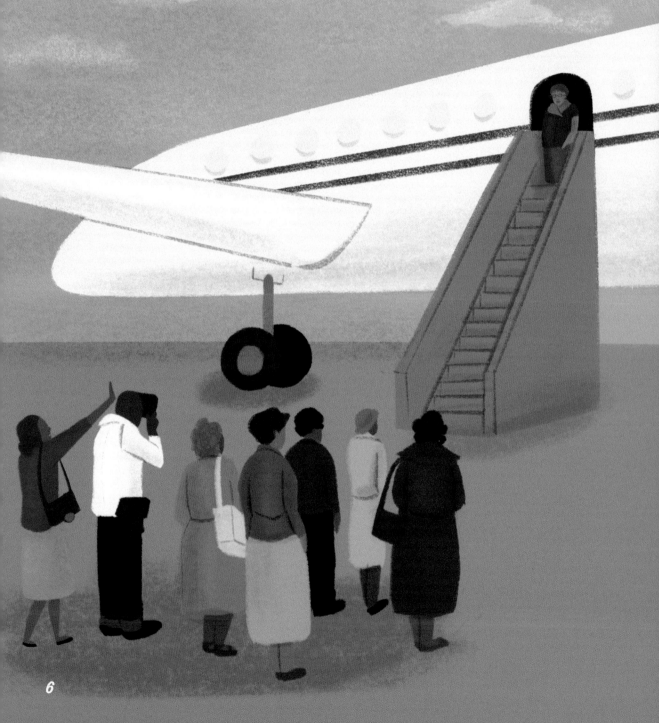

## Political Parties

In 1952, voters could join one of three political parties that best fit their beliefs. They were the Democratic, Republican, and Progressive parties. The Progressive Party wanted to end the Korean War and racial **discrimination**.

# DON'T FENCE ME IN

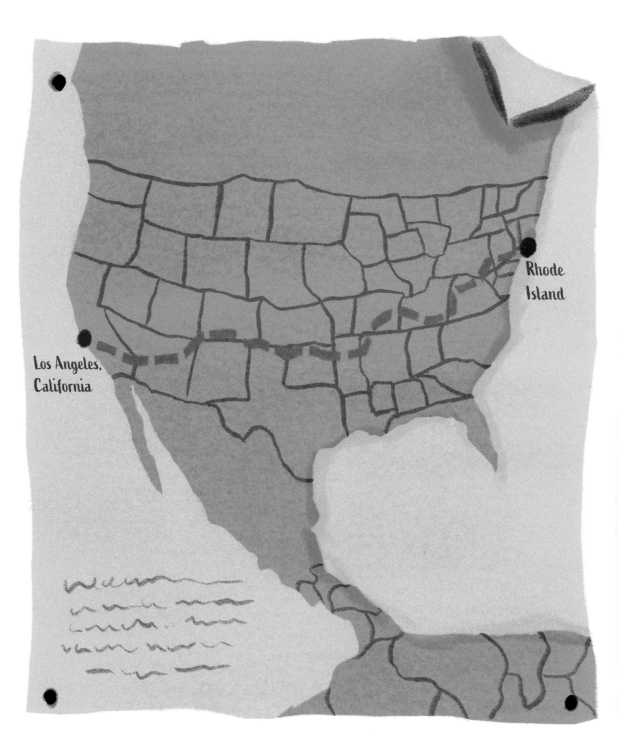

Los Angeles, California

Rhode Island

Charlotta was born in 1874 in Sumter, South Carolina. She grew up in the state of Rhode Island. Even when she was young, newspapers were important to Charlotta. After college, she went to work for a local Black newspaper, the *Providence Watchman*. There, she organized the paper's finances and tripled their ad sales.

In 1910, she moved from Rhode Island to Los Angeles, California. Many Black people in the United States were moving west at that time. They were looking for a better life. Together, they built schools, started businesses, and formed communities.

Charlotta's newspaper was flying off newsstands. She had been working there when she bought the press for $50 at an auction. She renamed it from the *Eagle* to the *California Eagle*. She didn't want her newspaper to be like others. She wanted to write about the good things that women and Black people were doing. She hired Joseph Blackburn Bass as an editor. Charlotta was becoming a leader in business and in **journalism**.

**WORKING TOGETHER**

Charlotta married Joseph Bass. Together, they grew the *California Eagle* from 4 pages to 20. They increased printing to 60,000 copies, more than any other African American newspaper on the west coast of the United States.

Charlotta's newspaper was her weapon. She waged war in print against housing discrimination, police **brutality**, and a lack of jobs for Black people. She wouldn't give up.

She **wrote articles...**

**...printed stories...**

**...and listened to people.**

1607
CALIFORNIA EAGLE
ESTABLISHED 1879
PRINTERS PUBLISHERS LINOTYPER

Charlotta ran for a seat on the Los Angeles City Council. Although she lost, she stayed true to her slogan: "Don't Fence Me In." People were proud to have her as their leader. Even people who disapproved of what she was doing could not fence her in.

# MANY KINDS OF BRAVERY

In the 1950s, it was considered "unladylike" to be outspoken. This was especially true for a Black woman. Charlotta was bold and brave. She wrote a weekly column, On the Sidewalk, about the lives of people in the Black community. It inspired her readers. The readers trusted her.

Charlotta brought the national "Don't Buy Where You Can't Work" **movement** to Los Angeles. Black people stopped shopping at stores that would not hire them. As a result, these stores made less money. This pressure made white businesses hire Black workers. It made some people angry.

Charlotta was brave in other ways, too. One night, a hate group called the Ku Klux Klan went to the newspaper office to scare Charlotta. Instead, she scared them away.

African Americans were told that life was better for them in Africa. They were told they should "go back home." Charlotta did not agree with the Back-to-Africa movement. She used her newspaper to deliver the message that Black people were American. They were here to stay!

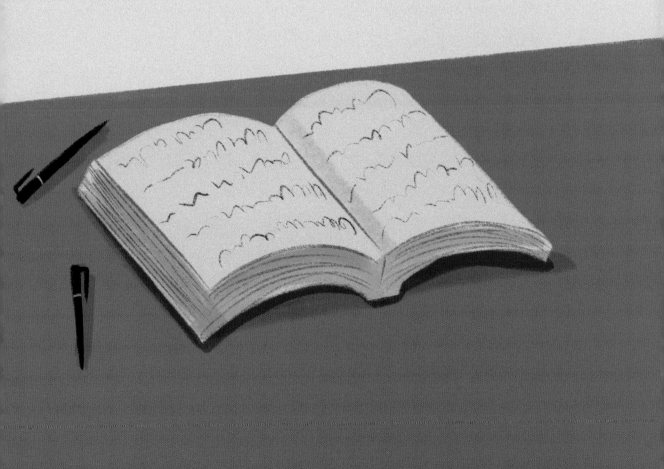

Charlotta was courageous on many levels. She was brave and fought against unfair rules. She stood up to hatred. She was brave to run for vice president in 1952. She was the first African American woman to be nominated for vice president. She did what others were afraid to do.

The Federal Bureau of Investigation (FBI) started watching Charlotta. They listened in on her phone calls. They wrote reports about her. They **accused** her of working against the United States. They tried to block her from publishing things they did not like in her newspaper.

Charlotta stopped working for the newspaper in 1951. In 1952, she ran for vice president with Vincent Hallinan, who wanted to be president. The Progressive Party did not win. However, she never stopped fighting for equal rights. She turned her garage into a community reading room. During election season, it doubled as a voter registration site. Charlotta wrote a book about her life, titled *Forty Years: Memoirs from the Pages of a Newspaper*.

**UNDER WATCH**

The FBI questioned Charlotta. They kept many files on her. They watched her until her death.

Charlotta died in 1969 at the age of 95. She was inducted into the California Hall of Fame in October of 2014 for her work in civil rights. Three years later, she was also inducted into the California Newspaper Hall of Fame. They honored Charlotta for being the managing editor of the *California Eagle* from 1912 to 1951. No matter what she did, Charlotta worked hard to make life easier in the future for others.

> **Here I could sit at the head of the table as a founding member, write my own program, a program for me and my people, that came from us.**
>
> —Charlotta Bass

# TIME LINE

**1874** Charlotta Amanda Spears is born on February 14th to Hiram and Kate Spears in Sumter, SC.

**1910** Charlotta moves from Rhode Island to California and begins working at the *Providence Watchmen* newspaper selling ads.

**1912** She purchases the *Eagle* newspaper, likely making her the first African American woman to own a newspaper. She renames it the *California Eagle* and hires Joseph Bass to be its new editor.

**1914** Charlotta marries Joseph Bass.

**1915** She brings the national "Don't Buy Where You Can't Work" movement to Los Angeles. It encouraged African Americans to spend their money at Black-owned businesses or businesses that hired African Americans.

**1945** Charlotta runs for Los Angeles City Council with the campaign slogan "Don't Fence Me In" but is unsuccessful.

**1951** Charlotta sells the *California Eagle* and moves to New York City.

**1952** Charlotta becomes the first African American woman nominated for vice president of the United States as a candidate of the Progressive Party. Her slogan is "Win or Lose, We Win by Raising the Issues."

**1960** Her autobiography, *Forty Years: Memoirs from the Pages of a Newspaper*, is published.

**1969** Charlotta dies in Los Angeles on April 12th and is buried in the Evergreen Cemetery alongside her husband. The grave marker lists only his name.

**2014** She is inducted into the 8th Class of the California Hall of Fame.

**2017** Charlotta is inducted into the California Newspaper Hall of Fame.

# GLOSSARY

**accused** (uh-KYOOZD): said that someone had done something wrong

**brutality** (broo-TAL-i-tee): extreme cruelty or violence

**convention** (kuhn-VEN-shun): a formal gathering of people who have the same interests

**discrimination** (dis-krim-i-NAY-shun): prejudice or unfair behavior to others based on differences in things such as age, race, or gender

**journalism** (JUR-nuh-liz-um): the work of gathering and reporting of news through newspapers, magazines, and other media

**movement** (MOOV-muhnt): a group of people working together to promote a cause

**nomination** (nah-muh-NAY-shun): the suggestion that someone would be the right person to do an important job or to receive an honor

**policy** (PAH-li-see): general plan or principle that people use to help them make decisions or take action

# INDEX

# TEXT-DEPENDENT QUESTIONS

1. How did Charlotta Bass come to own her newspaper?

2. How did Charlotta Bass use the *California Eagle* to help her community?

3. Which of the three political parties was Charlotta Bass a member of in 1952?

4. Why did Charlotta Bass encourage African Americans to stop buying at some department and grocery stores?

5. What is the name of Charlotta Bass's autobiography?

# EXTENSION ACTIVITY

Write down three things that concern you about your local community. Find a group near you that is working to help change one of these things. Find out what they do to help. What can you do to help them and improve your community? Make a list of three ways to make things better and do one of them.

# ABOUT THE AUTHOR

**J. P. Miller** Growing up, J. P. Miller loved reading stories that she could become immersed in. As a writer, she enjoys doing the same for her readers. Through the gift of storytelling, she is able to bring little- and well-known people and events in African American history to life for young readers. She hopes that her stories will augment the classroom experience and inspire her readers. J. P. lives in metro Atlanta and is the author of the *Careers in the US Military* and *Black Stories Matter* series.

# ABOUT THE ILLUSTRATOR

**Amanda Quartey** Amanda lives in the UK and was born and bred in London. She has always loved to draw and has been doing so ever since she can remember. At the age of 14, she moved to Ghana and studied art in school. She later returned to the UK to study graphic design. Her artistic path deviated slightly when she studied Classics at her university. Over the years, in a bid to return to her artistic roots, Amanda has built a professional illustration portfolio and is now loving every bit of her illustration career.

www.rourkeeducationalmedia.com

Quote source: Bass, Charlotta. "Acceptance Speech for Vice Presidential Candidate of the Progressive Party" (speech, 1952), Black Past, https://www.blackpast.org/african-american-history/1952-charlotta-bass-acceptance-speech-vice-presidential-candidate-progressive-party/.


Edited by: Tracie Santos
Illustrations by: Amanda Quartey
Cover and interior layout by: J.J. Giddings

**Library of Congress PCN Data**

Charlotta Bass / J. P. Miller
(Leaders Like Us)
ISBN 978-1-73164-890-7 (hard cover)
ISBN 978-1-73164-838-9 (soft cover)
ISBN 978-1-73164-942-3 (e-Book)
ISBN 978-1-73164-994-2 (ePub)
Library of Congress Control Number: 2021935434

Rourke Educational Media
Printed in the United States of America
01-1662111937